AF399761

NELSON MANDELA

The Fight Against Apartheid

Written by Françoise Puissant Baeyens
Translated by Rebecca Neal

NELSON MANDELA

- **Born:** 18 July 1918 in Mvezo (Cape Province).
- **Died:** 5 December 2013 in Johannesburg.
- **Main achievements:**
  - The fight against apartheid
  - The creation of Umkhonto we Sizwe ("Spear of the Nation"), the armed wing of the African National Congress (ANC), in 1960
  - Major contribution to the transition to democracy (1990-1994)
  - President of South Africa (1994-1998) following the country's first democratic elections
  - Key role in the reconciliation process

When Nelson Mandela was released from prison after 27 years on 11 February 1990, the eyes of the world were on South Africa. He was the most iconic figure in the fight against apartheid, the political regime established in 1948 which institutionalised racial segregation in all aspects of life in South Africa. Images of his release were broadcast across the world and inspired hope of a better future for the country.

When he left prison, his fist raised in a victory salute and welcomed by an enthusiastic crowd, his last speech before he was sentenced was at the forefront of everyone's minds:

> "I have fought against white domination, and I have fought against black domination. I have cherished the ideal of a democratic and free society in which all persons live together in harmony and with equal opportunities. It is an ideal which I hope to live for and to achieve. But if needs be, it is an ideal for which I am prepared to die." (*nelsonmandela.org*)

The extraordinary story of Nelson Mandela – who also went by the name Madiba, in homage to his ancestors' clan – was far from over. After his release, he played an important role in the negotiations between his party, the ANC, and the South African regime, which resulted in the dismantling of apartheid and the organisation of the country's first democratic elections. When he was elected president of the new "Rainbow Nation" in 1994, he faced the difficult task of leading South Africa down the long and bumpy road to reconciliation, assuaging the fears of the

country's white citizens and fulfilling the hopes
of its black citizens.

BIOGRAPHY

| Portrait of Nelson Mandela.

"TROUBLEMAKER"

Rolihlahla Mandela was born on 18 July 1918 in the village of Mvezo in the Bantustan of Transkei (Cape Province). Loosely translated, his first name means "pulling the branch of a tree", or more colloquially "troublemaker" in Xhosa. He had royal ancestry, as his father was a nobleman of the Thembu dynasty, one of the largest Xhosa tribes.

At the age of 7, he went to a Methodist school, making him the first member of his family to receive a formal education. When his father died two years later, he was taken in by the Thembu regent. In accordance with tradition, he was set to become an advisor to the future king.

At the age of 19, Mandela continued his education in another Methodist school in Fort Beaufort, before beginning his studies at the University of Fort Hare. However, he was expelled in his second year for taking part in a student protest. He then went back to his village, where another disaster awaited him: the King had chosen a fiancée for him. To escape this arranged marriage, he fled to Johannesburg in 1941.

JOINING THE ANC

Mandela's ambition was to become a lawyer. He took a correspondence course in law at the

University of Witwatersrand and obtained a position at a lawyers' firm thanks to Walter Sisulu (ANC leader, 1912-2003). This encounter had a decisive impact on his future: because of Sisulu, Mandela joined the ANC, a party founded to defend the interests of South Africa's black community. At this time, he also met Evelyn Mase (1922-2004), whom he married in 1944 and with whom he had four children.

His political career began in the same year, when he helped found the African National Congress Youth League. In the 1950s, Mandela rose to become a prominent figure within the party. However, his total commitment to his political cause led to the collapse of his first marriage.

In 1952, Mandela and Oliver Tambo (president of the ANC in exile, 1917-1993) founded the first black lawyers' firm in South Africa. The organisation was an immediate success and bolstered its founder's reputation.

In the summer of 1957, Mandela met a fellow ANC member, Winnie Madikizela (born in 1936), who was 16 years his junior. He fell in love with her, and married her a year after they first met.

They had two children together.

FIGHTING FOR FREEDOM

On 21 March 1960, a peaceful demonstration in Sharpeville was violently suppressed, leaving 69 people dead and around 180 injured. In the wake of the Sharpeville massacre, all the parties fighting apartheid, including the ANC, were outlawed, which meant that Mandela and the party's other leaders were driven underground.

Mandela was now convinced that armed struggle was necessary to defend his ideals. However, the members of Umkhonto we Sizwe, the ANC's newly created armed wing, were reluctant to cause human casualties, so they limited their activity to acts of sabotage.

After two years of underground activity, Mandela was captured in August 1962. A few months later, in 1963, most of the party's other leaders were also imprisoned. They were tried for high treason, found guilty and sentenced to life imprisonment.

IMPRISONMENT ON ROBBEN ISLAND

When he entered prison in 1964, Mandela was 46 years old. He did not regain his freedom until 27 years later, after spending 18 years at the notoriously brutal Robben Island prison off Cape Town. He became an increasingly well-known figure while he was in prison, and came to symbolise the struggle against the racist apartheid regime, which was increasingly condemned by the international community.

| Photograph of Mandela's prison cell on Robben Island.

In 1982, Mandela and his comrades were transferred to Pollsmoor Prison in Cape Town. Two years later, the Afrikaner government reached out to him and secret negotiations began.

PRESIDENT OF THE RAINBOW NATION

The ban on the ANC was lifted in 1990, and Mandela was released shortly afterwards. His release was met with jubilation across South Africa. The negotiations to lay the groundwork for a democratic state continued against a backdrop of constant clashes between the country's different racial communities.

NOBEL PEACE PRIZE

The efforts of Mandela and the South African president F. W. de Klerk (born in 1936) to abolish apartheid received international recognition, and in 1993 they were jointly awarded the Nobel Peace Prize.

With regard to his personal life, he separated from Winnie in 1992 and their divorce was finalised in 1996.

After South Africa's first democratic elections,

Mandela was elected president.

| Photograph of Mandela voting in the 1994 presidential election.

He spent his years as leader of the Rainbow

Nation working towards reconciliation. In 1999, at the end of his first term, he stepped down as president, but remained a highly respected figure in South Africa, with countless buildings, streets and public squares named after him.

AN INTERNATIONAL ICON

On his 80th birthday, he married Graça Machel (born in 1945), the widow of the former president of Mozambique.

DID YOU KNOW?

Mandela's last public appearance was during the 2010 World Cup final in Johannesburg. He had played a role in South Africa's successful bid to host the tournament.

From 2012 onwards, his health seriously deteriorated. His death on 5 December 2013 was met with a vast outpouring of grief as figures around the world paid tribute to the hero of South African reconciliation.

CONTEXT

It is impossible to understand the origins of the apartheid regime, which Mandela spent his entire life fighting against, without going back to the arrival of the first Europeans in South Africa.

THE SETTLING OF THE BOERS AND THE ARRIVAL OF THE BRITISH

In 1652, the Dutch East India Company established a trading post at the Cape of Good Hope. Farmers from the Netherlands gradually moved there in order to keep the post independent. Once they had achieved this goal, some of them returned home, while others decided to stay in the region indefinitely with the aim of climbing the social ladder and making their fortune. The Company allowed them to settle as free citizens: they were the first Boers (Dutch for "peasant").

In the late 18th century, the British landed in Cape Town and gradually took control of the region. The Boers, who were opposed to the introduction of the English language and legal system, settled in the neighbouring desert zones.

THE GREAT TREK

When the British decreed the abolition of slavery in 1833, the Boers saw this as a contravention of the divine order and decided to leave the Cape Town region. Their departure marked the beginning of the Great Trek, during which thousands of Boers, who wanted to throw off the yoke of colonial power, withdrew inland to found independent republics. This episode is considered to be the founding myth of their civilisation.

The native Africans were violently dispossessed of their property as the Boers, who saw themselves as the divinely ordained owners of the region, advanced inland.

THE EXPANSION OF THE BRITISH COLONY

The British also wanted to expand their territory, which resulted in a series of wars. The Boers were driven back once again, and then settled on the harsh plains of the Veld and founded the Orange Free State and Transvaal, which were both recognised as independent republics by the British in the 1850s.

Between 1866 and 1886, gold and diamond deposits were discovered in the heart of Transvaal and the previously poor rural region underwent a major wave of industrialisation. It became very wealthy and the first towns, such as Johannesburg, emerged.

In 1899, the Second Boer War broke out between the British, who wanted to get their hands on Transvaal's riches, and the Boers. After some initial setbacks, the British emerged victorious in 1902.

THE UNION OF SOUTH AFRICA

In 1910, the Union of South Africa was established. Although the country was a British dominion and had a Governor-General representing the monarch, it was run by a local government.

In 1913, the South African parliament passed the Natives Land Act, which meant that the country's black native majority could only own property in certain regions, covering just 10%

of the territory. These legal provisions laid the foundation for the future apartheid regime.

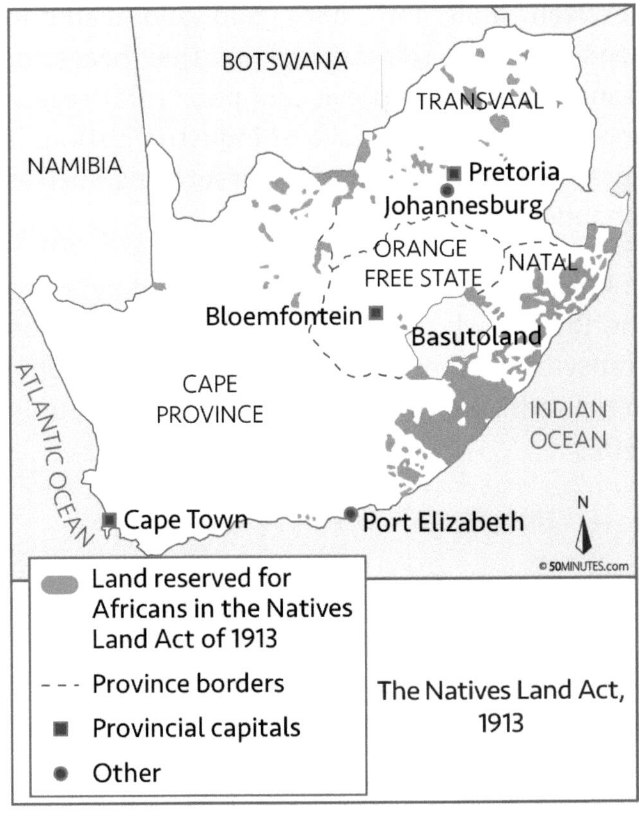

The Natives Land Act, 1913

One year later, the National Party was established. This was a nationalist party which aimed to provide political representation for the Afrikaners (a term which replaced "Boers" in the 20th century and referred to South Africa's non-English-speaking white population). It staunchly defended the idea that the Afrikaners had the sacred duty to make South Africa a white country.

<u>**DID YOU KNOW?**</u>

Afrikaner nationalism has its roots in the myth of the Boer peasants, who are presented as humble, devout pioneers, advancing into South Africa with nothing more than their guns, their bibles, some cattle and their wagons. The Afrikaans language, which evolved from Dutch and was mainly spoken by South Africa's non-English-speaking whites, also played a key role in forging a sense of identity within the group.

THE BIRTH OF CIVIL RIGHTS MOVEMENT

In response to the glaring inequalities between South Africa's white and black citizens, several movements were established to fight for the rights of the country's non-white communities. These included the African National Congress, which was founded in 1912 and fought for the emancipation of the black community. Its methods were initially inspired by those of the Indian National Congress, led by Mahatma Gandhi (Indian spiritual and political leader, 1869-1948).

GANDHI IN SOUTH AFRICA

Gandhi worked as a lawyer for an Indian firm in South Africa from 1893 to 1915. After witnessing the inequality and racism suffered by the country's black community, he founded the South African Indian Congress in 1895 and used nonviolent resistance and civil disobedience to work towards the organisation's goals.

THE BEGINNINGS OF APARTHEID

In 1948, the nationalist Daniel Malan (South African politician, 1874-1959) became prime minister. Apartheid was officially established, meaning that the pre-existing racial segregation was now enshrined in law. The country's population was classified into four main categories: Bantu (all black Africans), Coloured (those of mixed race), white and Asian (Indian and Pakistani). A series of laws deprived non-white citizens of their fundamental rights: for example, they were forbidden from marrying or having children with whites, voting, going on strike or forming trade unions.

In 1955, a Congress of the People took place in Kliptown and brought together several anti-apartheid political groups, including the ANC, the South African Indian Congress and the Communist Party. During the meeting, a Freedom Charter, which Mandela had helped to draft and which established the aim of creating a unified South Africa free of racial inequality, was adopted.

In 1960, nonviolent demonstrations were organised across the country in order to protest against passes (internal passports that non-white citizens were obligated to carry).

On 21 March 1960, when demonstrators gathered around the police station in the Sharpeville township (an urban area reserved for non-whites), the police officers responded by firing into the crowd. The government immediately declared a state of emergency and anti-apartheid parties, including the ANC, were declared illegal, forcing their leaders underground. Between 1962 and 1963, most of them were arrested and sentenced to life imprisonment.

STEVE BIKO AND THE BLACK CONSCIOUSNESS MOVEMENT

In the wake of the Sharpeville massacre, the anti-apartheid activist Steve Biko (1946-1977) founded the Black Consciousness Movement, which aimed to topple apartheid through the actions of black citizens alone. With Biko, a new generation of activists emerged and came to dominate the anti-apartheid struggle during the 1960s and 1970s, pushing Mandela and the ANC into the background.

In June 1976, in response to an appeal from Biko, demonstrations and popular uprisings took place in Soweto (a township of Johannesburg) in order to protest against the imposition of Afrikaans as the language of education. The demonstrations were brutally repressed by the police, with the estimated death toll standing at several hundred people, the majority of whom were students. One year later, Biko was arrested, and he died under unclear circumstances a month after his arrest. Subsequently, harsher sanctions were imposed on the country, which had already been heavily criticised, and it became a pariah within the international community.

THE END OF APARTHEID

The situation within the country was also deteriorating and the ANC, which was beginning to adopt more radical methods, carried out several bombings which claimed civilian victims. In the early 1980s, committees demanding Mandela's release emerged across South Africa, and citizens from all four corners of the globe rallied around the slogan "Free Nelson Mandela".

| Campaign in support of Mandela's release, dated 1988.

In this context, negotiations began between Mandela and the government. F. W. de Klerk, who became president in 1989, knew that the government's defence of apartheid was no longer tenable. As a result, on 2 February 1990 the ban on the parties fighting segregation was lifted, and a few days later he granted Mandela's unconditional release. Apartheid was officially abolished in 1991.

TOWARDS A DEMOCRATIC REPUBLIC

Negotiations continued against such a tense backdrop that many feared the outbreak of a civil war. Against all odds, the 1994 elections went smoothly, and Mandela became the first president of the new multiracial South Africa.

During his term, he worked to foster national unity and made massive political headway with the adoption of the new constitution in 1996. South Africa was able to emerge from apartheid with minimal violence, but the country still faced myriad other challenges, namely social inequality, poverty, crime and corruption.

HIGHLIGHTS

A PRAGMATIC IDEALIST

Mandela's move to Johannesburg marked the beginning of his career with the ANC. His new life in the city undoubtedly played a role in his decision to join the party, as Johannesburg's daily newspaper gave him a clearer view of the injustices facing black citizens.

Those who knew Mandela claim that his profound sense of morality was the driving force behind his fight. According to them, his integrity was one of his core values, and his sense of fairness, which was devoid of any political bias, allowed him to evaluation situations rationally and act pragmatically. This is emphasised by the South African writer André Brink (1935-2015), a friend and great admirer of Mandela, who claimed that "In the actions that marked and shaped Mandela's life, principle was always important, but never ideology" (in *The Guardian*, 1999).

Mandela's pragmatism and open-mindedness

are evidenced by his shift from African nationalism to non-racialism. When he joined the
ANC, the party's members were divided over
the question of whether or not it should allow
Asians, whites and Coloureds to join, or whether
membership should be limited to blacks only.
Unlike the ANC's old guard, Mandela was a firm
believer that the emancipation of black South
Africans could only be achieved through their
own efforts. In 1944, he was one of the founding
members of the African National Congress
Youth League, which was determined to radi-
calise the party leadership's position on this
issue. However, a few years later, the changing
situation on the ground forced him to reconsider
his stance. With the establishment of apartheid
and the growing inequality between whites and
non-whites, he became aware that, in order to
achieve the levels of mobilisation necessary
to combat the regime, the ANC would need to
work with other organisations. Mandela then
advocated a struggle in which all South Africans
would participate to build a unified, multiracial
society.

His decision to move away from pacifism in

1960, in the wake of the Sharpeville massacre, also speaks volumes about his character. He admitted that, for him, this decision was based on strategy rather than on any ideological precepts. After heated debates, Mandela managed to convince his partners in the ANC of the need for armed struggle. He would later write that "it is the oppressor who defines the nature of the struggle, and the oppressed is often left no recourse but to use methods that mirror those of the oppressor. At a certain point, one can only fight fire with fire" (in *Long Walk to Freedom*).

A CHARISMATIC FIGURE

Mandela's rise within the ANC was meteoric, and he soon established himself as a central figure within the party. His success can be largely explained by his personal charm and communication skills. In pictures from the time, his appearance is striking: he is tall, with an athletic build, an elegant appearance and a charismatic smile. His contemporaries were captivated by him, and he was particularly popular with women. However, his aura was not just due to his physical appearance. He also understood the power of symbols, as could be seen when he was photographed burning his pass in 1960, a bold gesture that highlighted his disdain for the authorities.

| Photograph of Mandela burning his pass, 1960.

He made another important symbolic statement when he appeared in a kaross, the traditional leopardskin cloak of Xhosa dignitaries, at the start of his trial in 1962. As early as the 1950s, when he was a successful lawyer and often dressed in a three-piece suit, he also allowed himself to be photographed in traditional garments. This was a way of showing the importance he attached to his African roots and to his illustrious lineage as part of the Thembu royal family. When he stood in the dock in his kaross, Mandela also drew attention to himself as a black man in a white man's court. He was fully aware of the power of this image and aimed to use it to leave a lasting impression on the trial's viewers.

A TRIAL THAT BECAME A POLITICAL FORUM

Mandela turned the Rivonia Trial (which took its name from the suburb of Johannesburg where the ANC representatives were arrested) into a political forum, and used his defence to assert his vision and his political ideals. He did not deny the crimes he was accused of, but refused to recognise the legitimacy of the authority judging him. This boldness is all the more impressive when we consider what was at stake in his trial: he was potentially facing the death penalty.

ROBBEN ISLAND AND THE BIRTH OF THE MANDELA MYTH

Mandela did not receive the death penalty; instead, he was sentenced to life imprisonment. However, far from breaking him, his years in prison made him into the man and leader he would later become.

He and his comrades refused to believe that they would die in prison, and this belief allowed them to keep their spirits up and endure the difficult conditions they faced on Robben Island. Mandela was always courteous to the Afrikaner prison guards, but he demanded and obtained respect in return.

He even thought that this "forced cohabitation" could be of benefit to him. He wanted to understand the Afrikaners, so he learnt their language in prison and took an interest in the history of the Boers. He realised that, in spite of the rift between their communities, the Afrikaners and his people had some similarities that could provide a starting point for dialogue and help bring about a reconciliation between the two groups. These included their nomadic, tribal, peasant past, their attachment to Africa and their struggle for survival.

Mandela also used his years in prison to study and to teach. He wanted the prison to have a university-like atmosphere, with each of his comrades sharing their knowledge with the others.

During this time, he became a symbol of the struggle against the white oppressor. As André Brink wrote, the fact that he was not physically there made his presence all the more strongly felt and helped turn him into a myth (in *Le Monde*, 2013). Mandela was aware that he had gradually become an icon, and allowed the ANC to use his image to mobilise the forces the party needed to regain its position as the leading organisation in the fight against apartheid.

As well as rallying people around the figure of Mandela, the ANC was also putting pressure on the government by taking more drastic action with its armed wing. It organised a series of bombings, one of which killed 19 people in Pretoria.

In the face of growing internal and international pressure, the government decided to make contact with Mandela, who by now had come to embody the fight against apartheid. The first meeting took place in Volks Hospital in Cape Town, where Mandela had been admitted for a prostate operation. When he was released, he was sent back to Pollsmoor, but now had a private room so that he could continue his secret discussions with the government. These negotiations were immensely risky, and Mandela was well aware of this. However, the risk paid off, as these talks paved the way for the negotiations that eventually led to the transition to democracy.

WINNIE MANDELA: A CONTROVERSIAL FIGURE

Winnie Mandela played a major role in the construction of the myth surrounding her husband, but as his release approached, she came to embody its darker side.

When Mandela was imprisoned, Winnie became his spokesperson. This new status gave her a great deal of visibility, which she used to publicly defy the authorities. As a result of her actions, she was subsequently harassed by the police, who arrested her and imprisoned her without trial on multiple occasions. She was tortured and placed in solitary confinement for long periods, but this only added to her reputation, as she remained loyal to her cause in the face of adversity.

After eight years of forced exile in the Orange Free State, Winnie returned to Soweto. However, this period of exile had left its mark on Mandela's wife, who was showing signs of radicalisation. In a 1986 speech, she justified necklacing (a punishment which involved putting a rubber tire around a suspected traitor's neck and setting it on fire), stating that this was how the country would achieve its liberation. She also established Mandela United Football Club, ostensibly a sports team but really a militia which spread terror in Soweto. Her reputation was permanently tarnished when a member of the club accused her of the murder of 14-year-old Stompie Moeketsi (1974-1989), an ANC activist whom she suspected of being a government informer.

Although some still saw her as the mother of the nation, many criticised her involvement in this murder. However, when Mandela was released from prison, he supported her, which allowed her to partially restore her reputation. Nonetheless, the couple no longer shared the same ideas and now struggled to understand one another. Their relationship deteriorated, and they separated in 1992. Even so, Winnie's popularity within the community allowed her to occupy a series of posts in the governments of Mandela and his successors.

MANDELA AT THE HEAD OF THE RAINBOW NATION

When Mandela was released, there was still a long way to go on the road to democracy and the transition looked set to be difficult. As a skilled diplomat, he realised that the white minority's power meant that he had to turn this community into an ally.

NEGOTIATIONS MARKED BY VIOLENCE

The Inkatha Freedom Party was violently opposed to any negotiations between the ANC and the government. This conservative, majority-Zulu party, which was founded in 1975, defended the idea of an ethnically and geographically separate Africa. The party's leader Mangosuthu Buthelezi (born in 1928) organised riots in 1992 which ended in massacres, particularly in Boipatong and Bisho. In spite of everything, the negotiations continued and were eventually successful.

Once he was leader of the country, Mandela carried out a number of symbolic acts of reconciliation. For example, he invited the wives of the country's former presidents and prime ministers to have tea with the wives of former Robben Island prisoners, and he publicly supported the Springboks at the 1995 Rugby World Cup, even though the team was closely associated with South Africa's white population. They went on to win the tournament.

Mandela knew that it would be difficult for his country to revisit the past, but he thought that it was a necessary step. Consequently, he set up the Truth and Reconciliation Commission to investigate human rights violations committed since the Sharpeville massacre in 1960. Both the victims and perpetrators of the crimes were encouraged to testify before the Commission, which was presided over by Archbishop Desmond Tutu (South African bishop, born in 1931). In exchange for their confessions, the perpetrators of the crimes received a full amnesty.

In line with his previously stated intentions, Mandela did not run for a second term. He dedicated the last years of his life to defending causes that were close to his heart, such as education and the fight against AIDS.

When he died at the age of 95, tributes to the hero of the anti-apartheid struggle and South Africa's first black president poured in from around the world. He received a state funeral, which was attended by a host of leading political figures. He was buried in Qunu, the village he had lived in as a child. In keeping with his wishes, his burial place is modest, with a single word carved on his gravestone: "Mandela".

- 49 -

IMPACT

THE END OF APARTHEID

Mandela's legacy is a South Africa in which apartheid has been laid to rest. As the South African author Mark Behr (1963-2015) has pointed out, the end of the segregationist regime also marked the disappearance of one of the last symbols of European colonialism.

While Mandela was always quick to insist that he was not solely responsible for bringing about change in the country, he was nonetheless the one who played the most decisive role in the battle, as his generosity of spirit ensured that the revolution took place without plunging the country into civil war.

A CHEQUERED POLITICAL RECORD

When he became president, Mandela's main focus was to consolidate national unity by working towards reconciliation between South Africa's different racial communities.

He delegated the management of current affairs to his vice-president – and future successor – Thabo Mbeki (born in 1942). Mbeki believed that the country's economic recovery depended on its reintegration into the global economic system dominated by the Western capitalist powers. Consequently, the ANC made a U-turn, leaving behind the Marxist influence that had guided its years of struggle and going down the path of liberalism. Once again, the organisation displayed the ideological pragmatism that it had already demonstrated on several occasions.

The country then enjoyed a period of economic growth, but Mbeki did not succeed in redistributing its wealth, in spite of some admirable efforts (the construction of new housing, improved electricity distribution and access to drinking water). The economic order which favoured whites was not really challenged, and racial segregation was replaced by social segregation which was still closely linked to the country's ethnic communities, even though a new black economic elite with strong ties to political power emerged. Mbeki's relationship with the entrepreneurial class was good, but he gradually lost touch with his popular base, which was left disappointed by the government's failure to solve the unemployment problem, to take measures to counter the spread of AIDS, and to halt the significant increase in crime and corruption. Some ANC representatives tried to effect change by adopting a more radical stance with a distinct anti-white flavour. Furthermore, the continuing inequality between black and white citizens resulted in some individual acts of revenge against the European community, which was deeply concerned about the situation.

Mbeki was accused of improper political infe-rence and forced to resign in 2008. A year later, Jacob Zuma (current president of South Africa, born in 1942) was elected president. Zuma, a representative of the left wing of the ANC, was able to capitalise on the disappointment of the country's poorest citizens with Mbeki's liberal economic policy. However, his reelection in 2014 took place against a backdrop of disillusionment. The country had yet to achieve economic and social equilibrium, in spite of the president's re-peated promises, and people from every sector of the population were losing faith in the ANC's political programme. Although the party still dominates South Africa's political landscape, it is not as popular as it once was.

THE FATHER OF THE NATION AND A UNIFYING FORCE

Mandela died over ten years after the end of his term as president, so he was around to witness the "post-Mandela" period.

Even after his retirement from politics, he was still an important public figure, as can be seen by his more or less permanent presence in the South African media. He remained equally prominent on the international stage. The ANC's problems did nothing to tarnish his image, and he was still universally acclaimed. It even seemed that, the more South Africa's political class was discredited in the eyes of its citizens, the more Mandela was held up as a hero, almost in spite of himself. Indeed, although he was aware of the myth surrounding him, he was always careful not to let a cult of personality develop.

It would be unfair to blame Mandela for the poor leadership of his successors. Nonetheless, his relative silence on the subject of his party's failings is striking. Apart from his admission that the ANC did not do enough to combat AIDS and his criticism of Mbeki's government for its failure to act, he remained completely loyal to the party.

The direct transition to democracy proved difficult, and it would take more than a few years to overcome the gross inequality resulting from 43 years of apartheid. As of yet, the ANC has not appeared to be up to the task, and the future of South Africa remains highly uncertain. However, even after his death, South Africans continue to rally around the figure of Mandela, and he remains an emblem with the power to inspire the moral rectitude needed to forge the new democracy.

SUMMARY

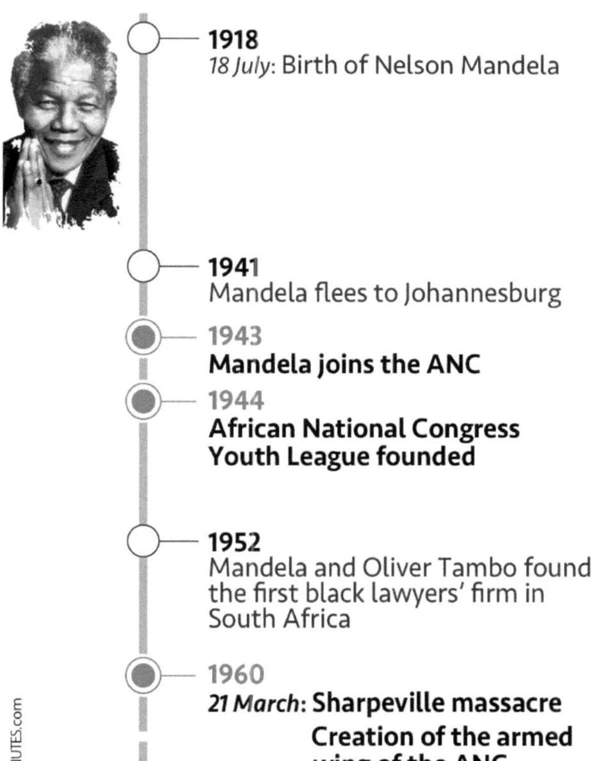

1918
18 July: Birth of Nelson Mandela

1941
Mandela flees to Johannesburg

1943
Mandela joins the ANC

1944
African National Congress Youth League founded

1952
Mandela and Oliver Tambo found the first black lawyers' firm in South Africa

1960
21 March: **Sharpeville massacre**
Creation of the armed wing of the ANC

- Nelson Mandela is an acclaimed figure around the world. He was a tireless anti-apartheid activist who spent 27 years in prison before becoming the pragmatic strategist behind the democratic process on his release. When he became president of South Africa, he worked towards reconciliation in a country still divided by the wounds of the past. After he stepped down from the presidency, he remained a revered figure and the embodiment of hope and reconciliation.

- Although he was an icon of the anti-apartheid struggle, Mandela resisted becoming the subject of a cult of personality. When he was released from prison, he addressed his fellow South Africans as follows: "I stand here before you not as a prophet but as a humble servant of you, the people. Your tireless and heroic sacrifices have made it possible for me to be here today. I therefore place the remaining years of my life in your hands" (cited in *The Guardian*, 2013).
- He was certainly not perfect: he was not a hero or a pacifist. In spite of this, we cannot help but be impressed by his qualities: his faith in humanity, his courage, his determination and his willingness to make sacrifices changed the destiny of South Africa.
- Today, Mandela's legacy is a cause for concern and questions. The inequality between South Africa's different ethnic communities persists,

with whites generally enjoying greater advantages, and some citizens feel left behind. For these people, Mandela forgave and gave up too much, and they feel betrayed. They criticise his clemency and the compromises he made to ensure a smooth transition to democracy, as they prevented real racial equality from being established.

- While this criticism may seem overly harsh, some other flaws are often ignored so as not to tarnish the myth surrounding Mandela. His party, the ANC, bears significant responsibility for South Africa's current problems, namely the ravages of the AIDS epidemic, rising crime rates and widespread corruption. Out of either loyalty or blindness, Mandela never criticised the ANC or seemed to accept that it could have made mistakes.
- In spite of South Africa's current difficulties, there is still hope that it could become the country that Mandela dreamed of and worked for. As André Brink wrote in 1999, "Nelson Mandela has achieved the impossible. It is now up to [his successors] to address the possible" (in *The Guardian*, 1999).

We want to hear from you!
Leave a comment on your online library
and share your favourite books on social media!

FIND OUT MORE

BIBLIOGRAPHY

- Behr, M. (2013) Nelson Mandela, une ligne morale. *Le Monde*. [Online]. [Accessed 14 November 2017]. Available from: <http://www.lemonde.fr/idees/article/2013/12/06/nelson-mandela-une-ligne-morale_3527090_3232.html>

- Beresford, D. (2013) Nelson Mandela obituary. *The Guardian*. [Online]. [Accessed 14 November 2017]. Available from: <https://www.theguardian.com/world/2013/dec/05/nelson-mandela-obituary>

- Brink, A. (1999) Mandela a tiger for our time. *The Guardian*. [Online]. [Accessed 14 November 2017]. Available from: <https://www.theguardian.com/world/1999/may/22/southafrica.nelsonmandela>

- Claude, P. (2013) Mort de Nelson Mandela, l'Africain capital. *Le Monde*. [Online]. [Accessed 14 November 2017]. Available from: <http://www.lemonde.fr/afrique/article/2013/12/05/nelson-mandela-est-mort_3427343_3212.html>

- Coquerel, P. (2010) *L'Afrique du Sud : une histoire séparée, une nation à réinventer*. Paris: Gallimard.

- Courrier International. (2010) *Mandela, un héros de notre temps*.

- Couzens, T., Coward, R., Frense, A. and Nicol, M. (2006) *Mandela, le portrait autorisé*. Paris: Acropole.

- Keller, B. (2013) Nelson Mandela, South Africa's Liberator as Prisoner and President, Dies at 95. *The New York Times*. [Online]. [Accessed 14 November 2017]. Available from: <http://www.nytimes.com/2013/12/06/world/africa/nelson-man-dela_obit.html?pagewanted=all>

- Le Monde. (2013) *Mandela : les discours entrés dans l'Histoire*. [Online]. [Accessed 14 November 2017]. Available from: <http://www.lemonde.fr/afrique/article/2013/12/06/mandela-les-discours-entres-dans-l-histoire_3526530_3212.html>

- Mandela, N. (1995) *Long Walk to Freedom*. London: Abacus.

- Mandelahistory.org. (No date) *Mandela: An Audio History*. [Online]. [Accessed 14 November 2017]. Available from: <http://www.mandelahistory.org/>

- Nelsonmandela.org. (2011) *"I am prepared to die"*. [Online]. [Accessed 14 November 2017]. Available from: <https://www.nelsonmandela.org/news/entry/i-am-prepared-to-die>

- Nelsonmandela.org. (No date) *Names*. [Online]. [Accessed 14 November 2017]. Available from: <https://www.nelsonmandela.org/content/page/names>

- Nelsonmandela.org. (No date) *The Nelson Mandela Centre of Memory*. [Online]. [Accessed 14 November 2017]. Available from: <https://www.nelsonmandela.org/>

- Sampson, A. (2011) *Mandela: The Authorised Biography*. New York: HarperCollins.

ADDITIONAL SOURCES

- Dubow, S. (2014) *Apartheid, 1948-1994*. Oxford: Oxford University Press.

- Fauré, M. (2017) *Apartheid*. Trans. Neal, R. Brussels: Plurilingua Publishing.

- Keller, B. (2013) *Tree Shaker: The Story of Nelson Mandela*. New York: Kingfisher Books.

- Lodge, T. (2003) *Politics in South Africa: from Mandela to Mbeki*. Oxford: James Currey Ltd.

- Mandela, N. (2010) *Conversations With Myself*. New York: Farrar, Straus and Giroux.

- Mandela, N. and Langa, M. (2017) *Dare Not Linger: The Presidential Years*. New York: Macmillan.

- Russell, A. (2009) *After Mandela, the Battle for the Soul of South Africa*. London: Hutchison.

- Sparks, A. (1996) *Tomorrow Is Another Country: The Inside Story of South Africa's Road to Change*. Chicago: University of Chicago Press.

- Sparks, A. (2009) *Beyond the Miracle: Inside the New South Africa*. Chicago: University of Chicago Press.

ICONOGRAPHIC SOURCES

- Portrait of Nelson Mandela. Royalty-free reproduction image.

- Photograph of Mandela's prison cell on Robben Island. Royalty-free reproduction image.

- Photograph of Mandela voting in the 1994 presidential election. Royalty-free reproduction image.

- Campaign in support of Mandela's release, dated 1988. Royalty-free reproduction image.

- Photograph of Mandela burning his pass, 1960. Royalty-free reproduction image.

FILMS AND DOCUMENTARIES

- *Mandela*. (1987) [TV movie]. Philip Saville. Dir. USA: Polymuse Productions, Titus Productions.

- *Mandela's Fight for Freedom*. (1995) [Documentary]. Stephen Clarke, Mick Gold and Stewart Lansley. Dirs. USA: Brian Lapping Associates.

- *Mandela*. (1996) [Documentary]. Angus Gibson

and Jo Menell. Dirs. SUA: Clinica Estetico, Island Pictures.

- *Mandela and de Klerk.* (1997) [TV movie]. Joseph Sargent. Dir. USA: Film Afrika Worldwide, Hallmark Entertainment, Showtime Networks.

- *The Long Walk of Nelson Mandela.* (1999) [Documentary]. Cliff Bestall. Dir. USA: Films2People.

- *Goodbye Bafana.* (1997) [Film]. Bille August. Dir. Germany/France/Belgium/South Africa/Italy/UK/Luxembourg: Banana Films, Arsam International, Film Afrika Worldwide, Future Films, Thema Production, X-Filme Creative Pool.

- *Invictus.* (2009) [Film]. Clint Eastwood. Dir. USA: Warner Bros.

- *Reconciliation: Mandela's Miracle.* (2010) [Documentary]. Michael Henry Wilson. Dir. USA: High Wire Productions.

- *Winnie.* (2011) [Film]. Darrell Roodt. Dir. South Africa/Canada: Ironwood Films, Equinoxe Films.

- *Mandela: Long Walk to Freedom.* (2013) [Film]. Justin Chadwick. Dir. UK/South Africa: Pathé, Videovision Entertainment, Distant Horizon, Origin Pictures.

COMMEMORATIVE BUILDINGS

- Nelson Mandela Metropolitan Art Museum, Port Elizabeth, South Africa.

- Nelson Mandela University, Port Elizabeth, South Africa.

- Statue of Nelson Mandela, unveiled in 2004 in Nelson Mandela Square in Sandton, Johannesburg.

- Statue of Nelson Mandela, unveiled in 2007 in Parliament Square, London.

- Statue of Nelson Mandela, unveiled in 2013 in the Union Building grounds, Pretoria.

ORGANISATIONS

- The Nelson Mandela Foundation, non-governmental organisation working to combat AIDS and improve education in South Africa.